FRANCIS FRITH'S

DOWN THE DART

PHOTOGRAPHIC MEMORIES

MARTIN DUNNING spent several years teaching before escaping the classroom to pursue a career as freelance writer. He has written for the 'Western Morning News' and the climbing magazine 'High', and is the author of several walking, travel and local history books. Martin has lived in Devon for over 40 years.

FRANCIS FRITH'S
PHOTOGRAPHIC MEMORIES

DOWN THE DART

PHOTOGRAPHIC MEMORIES

MARTIN DUNNING

First published in the United Kingdom in 2004 by
Frith Book Company Ltd

Limited Hardback Subscribers Edition Published in 2004
ISBN 1-85937-940-0

Paperback Edition 2004
ISBN 1-85937-859-5

British Library Cataloguing in Publication Data

Francis Frith's Down the Dart - Photographic Memories
Martin Dunning

Frith Book Company Ltd
Frith's Barn, Teffont,
Salisbury, Wiltshire SP3 5QP
Tel: +44 (0) 1722 716 376
Email: info@francisfrith.co.uk
www.francisfrith.co.uk

Printed and bound in Great Britain

Front Cover: **DARTMOUTH** *and Kingswear Castles c1875* 3146gt
Frontispiece: **POSTBRIDGE**, *The Old Clapper Bridge c1955*
P102005

*The colour-tinting is for illustrative purposes only, and is not intended
to be historically accurate*

AS WITH ANY HISTORICAL DATABASE THE FRITH ARCHIVE IS
CONSTANTLY BEING CORRECTED AND IMPROVED AND THE
PUBLISHERS WOULD WELCOME INFORMATION ON OMISSIONS
OR INACCURACIES

CONTENTS

FRANCIS FRITH
VICTORIAN PIONEER

FRANCIS FRITH, founder of the world-famous photographic archive, was a complex and multi-talented man. A devout Quaker and a highly successful Victorian businessman, he was philosophical by nature and pioneering in outlook.

By 1855 he had already established a wholesale grocery business in Liverpool, and sold it for the astonishing sum of £200,000, which is the equivalent today of over £15,000,000. Now a very rich man, he was able to indulge his passion for travel. As a child he had pored over travel books written by early explorers, and his fancy and imagination had been stirred by family holidays to the sublime mountain regions of Wales and Scotland. 'What lands of spirit-stirring and enriching scenes and places!' he had written. He was to return to these scenes of grandeur in later years to 'recapture the thousands of vivid and tender memories', but with a different purpose. Now in his thirties, and captivated by the new science of photography, Frith set out on a series of pioneering journeys up the Nile and to the Near East that occupied him from 1856 until 1860.

INTRIGUE AND EXPLORATION

These far-flung journeys were packed with intrigue and adventure. In his life story, written when he was sixty-three, Frith tells of being held captive by bandits, and of fighting 'an awful midnight battle to the very point of surrender with a deadly pack of hungry, wild dogs'. Wearing flowing Arab costume, Frith arrived at Akaba by camel sixty years before Lawrence of Arabia, where he encountered 'desert princes and rival sheikhs, blazing with jewel-hilted swords'.

He was the first photographer to venture beyond the sixth cataract of the Nile. Africa was still the mysterious 'Dark Continent', and Stanley and Livingstone's historic meeting was a decade into the future. The conditions for picture taking confound belief. He laboured for hours in his wicker dark-room in the sweltering heat of the desert, while the volatile chemicals fizzed dangerously in their trays. Back in London he exhibited his photographs and was 'rapturously cheered' by members of the Royal Society. His reputation as a photographer was made overnight.

VENTURE OF A LIFE-TIME

Characteristically, Frith quickly spotted the opportunity to create a new business as a specialist publisher of photographs. He lived in an era of immense and sometimes violent change.

For the poor in the early part of Victoria's reign work was exhausting and the hours long, and people had precious little free time to enjoy themselves. Most had no transport other than a cart or gig at their disposal, and rarely travelled far beyond the boundaries of their own town or village. However, by the 1870s the railways had threaded their way across the country, and Bank Holidays and half-day Saturdays had been made obligatory by Act of Parliament. All of a sudden the working man and his family were able to enjoy days out and see a little more of the world.

With typical business acumen, Francis Frith foresaw that these new tourists would enjoy having souvenirs to commemorate their days out. In 1860 he married Mary Ann Rosling and set out on a new career: his aim was to photograph every city, town and village in Britain. For the next thirty years he travelled the country by train and by pony and trap, producing fine photographs of seaside resorts and beauty spots that were keenly bought by millions of Victorians. These prints were painstakingly pasted into family albums and pored over during the dark nights of winter, rekindling precious memories of summer excursions.

THE RISE OF FRITH & CO

Frith's studio was soon supplying retail shops all over the country. To meet the demand he gathered about him a small team of photographers, and published the work of independent artist-photographers of the calibre of Roger Fenton and Francis Bedford. In order to gain some understanding of the scale of Frith's business one only has to look at the catalogue issued by Frith & Co in 1886: it runs to some 670 pages, listing not only many thousands of views of the British Isles but also many photographs of most European countries, and China, Japan, the USA and Canada - note the sample page shown on page 9 from the hand-written Frith & Co ledgers recording the pictures. By 1890 Frith had created the greatest specialist photographic publishing company in the world, with over 2,000 sales outlets - more than the combined number that Boots and WH Smith have today! The picture on the next page shows the Frith & Co display board at Ingleton in the Yorkshire Dales (left of window). Beautifully constructed with a mahogany frame and gilt inserts, it could display up to a dozen local scenes.

POSTCARD BONANZA

The ever-popular holiday postcard we know today took many years to develop. In 1870 the Post Office issued the first plain cards, with a pre-printed stamp on one face. In 1894 they allowed other publishers' cards to be sent through the mail with an attached adhesive halfpenny stamp. Demand grew rapidly, and in 1895 a new size of postcard was permitted called the court card, but there was little room for illustration. In 1899, a year after Frith's death, a new card measuring 5.5 x 3.5 inches became the standard format, but it was not until 1902 that the divided back came into being, so that the address and message could be on one face and a full-size illustration on the other. Frith & Co were in the vanguard of postcard development: Frith's sons Eustace and Cyril continued their father's monumental task, expanding the number of views offered to the public and recording more and more places in Britain, as the

coasts and countryside were opened up to mass travel.

Francis Frith had died in 1898 at his villa in Cannes, his great project still growing. The archive he created continued in business for another seventy years. By 1970 it contained over a third of a million pictures showing 7,000 British towns and villages.

FRANCIS FRITH'S LEGACY

Frith's legacy to us today is of immense significance and value, for the magnificent archive of evocative photographs he created provides a unique record of change in the cities, towns and villages throughout Britain over a century and more. Frith and his fellow studio photographers revisited locations many times down the years to update their views, compiling for us an enthralling and colourful pageant of British life and character.

We are fortunate that Frith was dedicated to recording the minutiae of everyday life. For it is this sheer wealth of visual data, the painstaking chronicle of changes in dress, transport, street layouts, buildings, housing, engineering and landscape that captivates us so much today. His remarkable images offer us a powerful link with the past and with the lives of our ancestors.

THE VALUE OF THE ARCHIVE TODAY

Computers have now made it possible for Frith's many thousands of images to be accessed almost instantly. Frith's images are increasingly used as visual resources, by social historians, by researchers into genealogy and ancestry, by architects and town planners, and by teachers involved in local history projects.

In addition, the archive offers every one of us an opportunity to examine the places where we and our families have lived and worked down the years. Highly successful in Frith's own era, the archive is now, a century and more on, entering a new phase of popularity. Historians consider the Francis Frith Collection to be of prime national importance. It is the only archive of its kind remaining in private ownership. Francis Frith's archive is now housed in an historic timber barn in the beautiful village of Teffont in Wiltshire. Its founder would not recognize the archive office as it is today. In place of the many thousands of dusty boxes containing glass plate negatives and an all-pervading odour of photographic chemicals, there are now ranks of computer screens. He would be amazed to watch his images travelling round the world at unimaginable speeds through internet lines.

The archive's future is both bright and exciting. Francis Frith, with his unshakeable belief in making photographs available to the greatest number of people, would undoubtedly approve of what is being done today with his lifetime's work. His photographs depicting our shared past are now bringing pleasure and enlightenment to millions around the world a century and more after his death.

THE RIVER DART
AN INTRODUCTION

THE DART is not a big river. It flows for only about forty miles, and the 425 square miles of its drainage basin are home to a mere 40,000 people. The measure of a river's greatness, however, lies not in bald statistics but in the stories it can tell - stories of the people who live on its banks, who navigate its waters, and whose lives are inextricably tied to the moody beast that flows past their doorsteps, sparkling and tranquil one day, swollen and spiteful the next. They are fishermen and ferrymen, miners and merchants, farmers, wool combers, cobblers and shipwrights; there is a supporting cast of ships, livestock, sea trout and salmon, and a stage carved from granite, limestone and slate.

The Dart rises on the bleak plateau of Dartmoor, the East Dart on the slopes of Cut Hill and the West Dart below Whitehorse Hill. Here, 1,800 feet up, it may rain for half the year. The underlying granite is hard and impervious, and the rainfall is sucked up by the thick blanket of peat bog that covers the landscape. Even the sponge-like bog gives up its water to gravity, however, and soon the stagnant, tea-coloured water becomes a trickle and eventually a stream. Other streams join the fledgling rivers: Summer Brook joins the West Dart, and Conies Down Brook the East, and very soon they are both happily gurgling their way south and east.

Salmon fry, making their way downstream from the spawning grounds where their parents expired after their epic struggle upstream, share the water with tiny brown trout and frogs. Dippers and the occasional heron patrol the shallows, and overhead buzzards and ravens soar while the wind sighs through the cotton grass and heather. The landscape appears to be a natural, eternal wilderness, but even here the hand of man is evident. Four thousand years ago the land was forested, and only attained its present treeless state after Bronze Age man, whose stone rows, burial mounds and hut circles still dot the hillsides, felled the trees. Wistman's Wood, on the West Dart, is one of the few pieces of woodland that survived.

Some of this felling was done to clear land for livestock, but an equal amount was to provide fuel for the moor's first industry. In the bed of the streams lay black rocks, cassiterite, the ore of tin, washed down from the mother veins; Bronze Age man was the first in a long line of miners to exploit this metal, which was to be the foundation on which towns like Ashburton built their wealth.

The East Dart meets civilisation for the first time at Postbridge and the West Dart at Two Bridges, and both places mark a change in the character of the river. Gone is the yellow bleakness of the open moorland, to be replaced by sheltered valleys in which grow rowan, hawthorn and scrub willow, and bounded by walled fields where cattle and sheep graze. Here, too, are the first bridges; ancient clapper bridges such as those at Postbridge, and delightful humpbacked bridges like the one at Huccaby.

By the time the East and West Dart unite they have both picked up more tributaries and are powerful rivers in their own right, capable, when in flood, of shifting even the massive granite slabs of clapper bridges. After Dartmeet the combined flow plunges pell-mell into what is the most spectacular section of the Dart, the gorge that runs down to Holne Bridge. The valley here is deep and narrow; from the lofty heights of Bench Tor and Mel Tor, facing each other across a bend in the river a mere half mile apart, there is a drop of over four hundred feet down steep,

oak-clad hillsides to the river. The water here roars and boils around mossy boulders; it races down rapids and cascades, and drops in misty sheets down steps in the valley floor, eager to shake off the restricting squeeze of the gorge.

For nearly eight miles below Dartmeet the river races, barely seen by the hordes of tourists, past Deadman's Corner, and past Buckland Bridge, where the Webburn joins in to swell the flow; then past Lover's Leap and Raven Rock until eventually, just below Holne Bridge, it begins to tire of all that youthful exuberance and settles into a more stately progress through less dramatic, agricultural countryside. In the twenty miles - half its total length - it has flowed from its source high on the moor, the river has lost 1,600ft in altitude, gathered seven major tributaries and twice that number of smaller ones, and has left behind the granite that was its birthstone. The Dart is no longer a moorland river.

A few miles below Holne Bridge the Dart encounters its first settlements of any size: Buckfast and Buckfastleigh. Both owe their prosperity to their situation on the river, for the ready power it supplied and the softness of its water

TOTNES, *From the Exeter Road 1931* 84018

allowed the growth of a thriving woollen industry. Wool from the thousands of sheep that grazed the moors to the north-west, and the rich farmland of the South Hams, was sheared, combed, carded, spun and eventually woven into the robust Devon cloth that made many a fortune.

At Dart Bridge - the first on our journey to be built from limestone rather than the previously ubiquitous granite - the Dart is joined by another of its tributaries, the Ashburn, from which Ashburton takes its name. Ashburton lies three miles up the valley, and its wealth, accumulated earlier than that of Buckfastleigh, was based on tin. In 1285 Edward I granted Ashburton the status of Stannary Town, a decision that was to ensure its prosperity for several centuries. Tin from the east of the moor was assayed and stamped at Ashburton, that from the west of the moor went to Tavistock, and any disputes were sorted out at the Stannary Parliament which met at Crockern Tor.

Just downstream from Dart Bridge is the first new bridge on the river, the modern concrete structure that carries the A38, and from here to Totnes the river is accompanied by the South Devon Railway, still operating steam trains. The valley here is broad, flat and pastoral; cattle graze contentedly, and the hillsides are dotted with fine Devon farmsteads such as Hood Manor and Riverford Farm.

At Staverton the industrial theme re-emerges, with a magnificent old mill building standing next to the medieval bridge, after which another four tranquil miles through farmland leads to the weir at Totnes. As we all learned in our geography lessons, a river passes typically through three stages on its journey to the sea: the youthful river, babbling its way down from the uplands, as the Dart does between its source and Holne Bridge; the mature river, flowing steadily and purposefully; and the old river, meandering lazily along a broad flood plain. This last phase of old age is denied to the Dart, as it is to all South Devon's rivers, by a trick of geological history. At the end of the last Ice Age sea levels here rose, inundating the lower parts of the river valleys and forming rias, flooded estuaries that reach far inland. The weir at Totnes marks the end of the mature section of the Dart, and a fundamental change in the river's nature, for below here everything is governed by the tides.

Totnes is the lowest bridging point on the Dart, and the highest point to which ocean-going ships can sail, factors which firstly dictated the founding of Totnes, to defend the river crossing, and later ensured its prosperity as a centre of trade, particularly in cloth. Above Totnes the river, while providing a living for the tinners and mill owners, presented a barrier to travel, but downstream from Totnes it was the only way to travel. Steamer Quay, Town Quay and later Baltic Wharf have, over the centuries, seen every imaginable type of cargo, passenger and livestock coming and going. Around the town are indicators of the importance of the river to the life of Totnes: on the Plains is a pub called the Dartmouth, while the name Steamer Quay needs no explanation. Baltic Wharf is a reference to the timber trade with Scandinavia, and to the west is the evocatively named Fishcheaters' Lane, so called because it was used to avoid paying duty on salmon.

Salmon provided a living from the river for hundreds of years, and the fisheries of Ashprington and Stoke Gabriel are mentioned in the Domesday Book, but there were other harvests to be gathered from the Dart. Shellfish, particularly cockles, were a staple part of the diet for those unable to afford salmon, and the warm, sheltered valley was an ideal spot for growing fruit, most famous of which were the 'Ditsum plums'. The bed of the river provided a living for some: fine grained sand, washed down over the millennia from Dartmoor, was much in demand for building, and dredging also helped keep the channel free for the ships that plied up and down the estuary.

The river winds and jinks its way from Totnes towards the sea down a wooded valley whose shores are broken by mysterious little creeks and dotted with villages and farms. Every settlement has its own quay, used today mainly by the tourist industry, but in times past vital to the trade and travel of everyday life: passengers, pots and pans, livestock, timber, lime, sand, salmon and shellfish. As the estuary broadens it becomes busier, and finally, passing Old Mill Creek to starboard, our passage brings us to Dartmouth.

Sheltered from the full force of the Atlantic westerlies by a narrow harbour entrance, and providing deep water anchorages for ships of up to 500ft, Dartmouth has a proud maritime history. It was from here, in 1147, that 164 ships departed for the Second Crusade. In the 13th and 14th centuries Dartmouth grew rich, exporting cloth and dried fish to Bordeaux and importing wine, and by the 16th century the town's fishermen were braving the vastness of the Atlantic to fish the Grand Banks off Newfoundland. The decision to build the naval dockyard at Plymouth rather than Dartmouth was a setback to the town's ambitions, and so was losing the mail ship service to Southampton, but the busy port weathered its misfortunes; it made its latest great contribution to history in 1944, when it was one of the ports from which the D-Day armada set sail. Today, Dartmouth's great days as a trading port and seat of exploration are behind it, but the ferries still bustle to and fro, the streets are thronged with visitors, and the marinas welcome sailors from all over the world; the Dart is still the lifeblood of the town.

Beyond is nothing but sea and the rest of the world. The salmon fry slip silently out between the castles at the mouth of the estuary, heading for the Atlantic to grow fat and sleek before returning to perpetuate the cycle of life that begins, as does the Dart itself, on the windswept plateau of the moor.

DARTMOUTH, *The 'Hindostan' and HMS 'Britannia' 1889* 21598

POSTBRIDGE TO BUCKFASTLEIGH

POSTBRIDGE, *The Old Clapper Bridge c1960*
P102002

Clapper bridges are unique to Dartmoor, and this one over the East Dart is one of the best preserved. Clappers are thought to have been built in the 13th and 14th centuries by miners and farmers. Each of the spanning slabs measures 6ft by 12ft and weighs 8 tons.

POSTBRIDGE
The Old Clapper Bridge c1955
P102005

A few miles north of Postbridge is Devon's great watershed. Just below Whitehorse Hill, and within half a mile of each other, rise the East Dart and the Taw, one flowing to the English Channel and the other to the Bristol Channel.

TWO BRIDGES, *The Hotel c1955* T153009

Crockern Tor, a mile to the north, is the site of the Devon Stannary Parliament which sat from 1305 to 1749. Two Bridges is at the junction of all the ancient packhorse trails that cross the moor, and was thus the obvious meeting place for miners from all points of the compass.

▶ **HEXWORTHY**
The Forest Inn
c1955 H240001

The original pub here on the West Dart was a typical thatched Dartmoor cottage, built in 1830. The present structure was built in 1914 after a fire and has seen some (in)famous visitors - the Kray twins and Charlie Richardson all stayed here.

◀ **HEXWORTHY**
Huccaby Bridge
c1955 H240004

There has been a bridge here for hundreds of years, but the present one was built in the early 19th century. 9ft wide, and with a central span of 9 yards, it is typical of moorland bridges in that it boasts cutwaters, pointed extensions to the bridge piers, designed to deflect the flow of the river in flood.

▲ **DARTMEET,** *On the East Dart c1871* 5529

To reach Dartmeet in 1871, carrying a cumbersome Victorian camera and the paraphernalia that accompanied it, would have been something of an adventure. Coaches ran from hotels such as the Dolphin at Bovey Tracey, and passengers would have had to endure several hours on tooth-looseningly rough roads.

◄ **DARTMOOR**
The River Dart, Dartmeet 1890 25948

The life of a moorland farmer is tough today; in 1890, with no Landrovers, electricity or modern waterproofs, it must have been unimaginably harsh and very isolated. The great blizzard of 1891 would have left communities like this inaccessible for weeks or even months.

◄ **DARTMEET**
The Clapper Bridge
1925 78520

The story of this clapper illustrates the power of the Dart in flood. Despite the fact that the spans weigh several tons, the bridge was swept away in a flood in 1826 and rebuilt in the 1840s. Soon after, another flood wreaked havoc. A further restoration took place in 1888 before the bridge was damaged again in 1910.

◀ **DARTMOOR**
Dartmeet Bridge
1890 25947

The original crossing here was a ford, probably used since Bronze Age times. The present bridge bears a plaque inscribed 'County Bridge 1792'. On the left, the river bank is being cultivated as a vegetable garden - essential when the nearest shop is several hours away.

▲ **DARTMEET,** *The Meeting of the East and West Dart Rivers 1890* 25945

The nearest church is at Widecombe, which meant a long walk for worshippers and a mighty task for coffin bearers. A little way up the hill from where this picture was taken is the coffin stone, where the cortege traditionally stopped for a breather before resuming their long trudge.

◀ **DARTMEET**
General View 1925
78514

It is a mere 35 years on from picture 25945, but how things have changed: the age of the car has arrived, and telegraph poles now line the roadside. As a result of improved access and communications, Dartmeet is no longer so isolated, and the hamlet has grown.

19

DARTMEET
The River Dart from the Bridge c1935
D5025

This gathering of cars shows the brief flowering of the tourist industry in the thirties. Very soon petrol rationing would bite, and a sight like this would not be seen again until the early fifties.

HOLNE, *Near Bench Tor c1871* 5523

The long north-south ridge that leads to Bench Tor is one of the finest spots for a view of the gorge below Dartmeet. Shown on old maps as Benjy Tor, it was described by John Lloyd Warden Page in 1892 as 'clothed with dwarf wood, and green with mosses'.

DARTMOOR
The River Dart,
New Bridge 1890
25954

The first bridge here was built in the 15th century, and by 1645 it had fallen into serious disrepair. Sir Thomas Hele visited the bridge with a group of Justices, who ordered that £13 be raised for repairs - an early example of road tax.

THE RIVER DART, *The View below Holne Chase c1870* 5532

After a particularly hair-raising experience near here in 1890, J L W Page wrote: '... let me sound a note of warning about the Dart. I do not think that the ordinary tourist has any idea of the dangerous nature of this impetuous river, or of the risk that is run in attempting to ford its treacherous current.'

THE CONFLUENCE OF THE DART AND THE WEBBURN RIVERS *c1871* 5531

The East and West Webburn Rivers drain the area round Widecombe before joining at Lizwell Meet and flowing on to join the Dart just below Buckland Bridge. The hillside on the right shows signs of having been cleared by foresters, who at this time would have used shire horses to move the timber.

HOLNE CHASE, *Lover's Leap c1870* 5534

'The name is suicidal, and they tell you that a pair of desperate lovers actually did cast themselves in the pool below, but as no one seems to know who they were, I, for one, venture to doubt the story.' So wrote J L W Page in 1892. He obviously was not a romantic.

DARTMOOR, *The Upper Dart, the View from Upper Buckland Drive 1890* 25961

The Buckland Drives, following the rim of the flatter land high up on the eastern bank of the Dart, were very popular during the 19th century. Coaching inns such as the Dolphin at Bovey Tracey ran regular excursions.

▼ **HOLNE,** *The Dart Valley 1890* 25965

The steep, densely wooded gorge below Dartmeet is a wild, inaccessible place, and farmers, exhibiting their usual good sense, have never tried to cultivate it. The surrounding hills are high and the climate damp, but the land has good grazing and can even be prevailed upon to produce a good crop of hay – note the hayrick on the left.

► **HOLNE**
The Village
c1960 H101006

Holne has a fine pub - the Church House Inn - and a famous son in Charles Kingsley, author of 'The Water Babies' and 'Westward Ho!', who was born in 1819 in the vicarage while his father was curate.

◄ HOLNE
The River Dart,
Holne Bridge
c1871 5521

The jump into the deep pool on the downstream side of the bridge was a popular activity. It usually involved several minutes teetering on the parapet trying to summon up the courage, and the water, when you hit it, was very cold, believe me!

► HOLNE
The View from the
Bridge c1871 5522

Holne Bridge marks the end of 'The Loop', a two-mile passage of white water canoeing which starts at New Bridge, and is only paddleable in winter when the river is in flood. The last section of rapids seen here is mild by comparison with the excitement of Lover's Leap (picture 5534, page 22).

► **ASHBURTON**
General View c1955
A67031

Ashburton lies in the valley of the River Ashburn, which joins the Dart at Buckfastleigh. In 1258 it was declared a Stannary Town by Edward I, a status which allowed it a measure of autonomy, with important decisions being made by the Stannary Parliament at Crockern Tor.

◄ **ASHBURTON**
The Bull Ring,
East Street 1904
51204

A fine selection of Edwardian pinafores, knickerbockers and caps is on display here. Photographers would have been a comparative rarity in 1904; this, combined with the long exposure required, probably accounts for the rather 'posed' nature of the picture.

▲ **ASHBURTON,** *East Street 1913* 65277

Bull baiting is recorded in Ashburton as far back as 1174 and, you would imagine, posed a serious threat to life and limb in such a confined space. The fine granite monument which marked the spot has long since fallen victim to the demands of traffic flow. The butcher's shop on the left advertises 'New Season Lamb: Easter Dainty Dish'.

◀ **ASHBURTON**
West Street 1913 65278

Cove's London Hotel (centre left) is now the Moorish Wine Bar, and J H Easterbrook's Boot and Shoe Warehouse (left) is now two separate businesses. Prices of shoes in 1913 ranged from 1s 11d to an exorbitant 3s 6d!

ASHBURTON
The Bullring 1913
65279

The slate-hung building (second left) was once a gaming house, and is still known as the Card House. The frontage has the suits of a pack of cards carved into the slates. The Capital and Counties Bank (centre) is now Lloyds TSB.

▲ **ASHBURTON,** *North Street 1936* 87480

The building on the right with the granite arch is now A R Church, an ironmonger's, but was once the Mermaid Inn and played host to the Parliamentarian General Fairfax during the Civil War. The Town Hall (centre left, with the bell tower) was built by Lord Clinton in 1850 to replace the wooden 16th-century structure which stood at the Bull Ring.

◀ **ASHBURTON**
West Street c1960
A67035

Off West Street, behind Sparnham House, was the site of one of Ashburton's two umber mines - the only ones in the country. Umber was used as a pigment in the paper and cloth industries, but demand died out and the mines shut in the early part of the 20th century, only to receive a new lease of life during World War II when umber was used for camouflage paint.

ASHBURTON, *West End c1955* A67029

Ashburton was the terminus of the nine-mile branch of the Buckfastleigh,
Totnes and South Devon line, which was completed in 1872. The last passenger
train ran in 1958, but there was a brief renaissance when the Dart Valley
Railway took over the line. However, the construction of the new A38 on the
track called time on the railway, and the very last train ran on 2 October 1971.

► **BUCKFAST**
St Mary's Abbey 1922
73190

In 1882 a group of French Benedictines re-established a community here. In 1907, in an act of quite astonishing faith and tenacity, the six monks started to build a new abbey. Only one monk had any stone working skills, but that did not deter them. Here, the abbey is almost complete save for the tower.

◄ **BUCKFAST**
The Abbey and the Moor
c1965 B636042

Buckfast, a mile up the Dart valley from Buckfastleigh, was home to a community of Cistercian monks from the 10th century. The original monastery fell prey to Henry VIII's dissolution of the monasteries in 1539, and a hiatus of 350 years ensued before the monks returned.

► **BUCKFAST**
*Buckfast Abbey
c1955* B636023

The abbey, built from locally quarried limestone, was finished in 1938, shortly before the death of Abbot Anscar Vonier, who had been the driving force behind the construction. The 158ft tower was the last part to be erected (see picture 73190 for comparison).

◄ **BUCKFASTLEIGH**
The Church c1955
B238014

Holy Trinity, built between the 13th and 15th centuries, was hit by a devastating fire on the night of 21 July 1992. Seven fire crews attended, but as the church is high on a hill, water had to be pumped from the valley below. By the time the fire was out, the church was a shell, although the tower survived.

▲ **BUCKFASTLEIGH,** *The Bridge, Station Road c1960* B238017

Church Bridge, also known as Harps Bridge, was built in 1749 and crosses the River Mardle. From here, 196 steps run up the hill to Holy Trinity Church, nearly 300ft above sea level. Reaching the church from the Dart valley to the north is no easier, as it involves climbing a very steep track called Fairies' Hill.

◀ **BUCKFASTLEIGH**
General View c1955
B238020

Probably taken from somewhere near Loverscombe, this shows the old A38 (centre) before the dual carriageway was built in the 1970s. The new road takes the land to the right of centre, and is only a few yards away from the apex of the obvious bend. The old road still marks the boundary of Dartmoor National Park.

◄ **BUCKFASTLEIGH**
The Bridge over the River Dart c1955
B238024

Dart Bridge is the first on the river to be built from anything other than granite - its four arches are constructed from local limestone. The A38 is now carried by a modern concrete bridge 200 yards downstream, and the tea shack (centre) has gone, to be replaced by a Little Chef which occupies the area just out of the picture on the right.

◄**BUCKFASTLEIGH**
The Bridge over the River Dart c1960
B238026

This bridge is first recorded as 'Dertebrygg' on the Assize Rolls of 1356; since then it has been enlarged several times as traffic has grown heavier. In 1809 it was only 8ft 6ins wide; by 1926 the width had grown to 19ft, and in 1938 its final widening left it at 40ft.

◄**BUCKFASTLEIGH**
The River Dart c1960 B238025

The chimney in the background (right) is that of Berry's or Lower Mill, the last remnant of a once thriving industry. In 1964 it was producing 4,000 blankets every week, but the rise in popularity of the duvet put paid to that, and the mill turned to producing yarn for carpets. The chimney was demolished in 1979, but the Buckfast Spinning Company is still on the site.

BUCKFASTLEIGH
Fore Street c1965
B238062

Buckfastleigh was for centuries the centre of the South Devon cloth industry, as its location on the Dart meant there was a ready source of power. So influential was the town that the Abbot of Buckfast was a member of the Totnes Merchants' Guild.

BUCKFASTLEIGH, *The White Hart Hotel c1965* B238066

The White Hart is over 400 years old, and spent the first 200 years of its life as one of the town's many woollen mills. As the wool trade declined, the mill closed, and a pub was built on the site, originally called the Fleece and eventually the White Hart.

▲ BUCKFASTLEIGH
On the River Mardle 1931 84043

The Mardle rises several miles to the east, near the summit of Ryder's Hill, which at 1,689ft is the highest point on the south moor. After flowing through Buckfastleigh, the Mardle joins the Dart above Austin's Bridge.

◀ *detail from* 84043

HOOD BRIDGE TO TOTNES

TOTNES, *Hood Bridge 1905* 53219

Also known as Riverford Bridge and Emmet's Bridge, this carries the A384. Despite its narrowness and medieval-style recesses for pedestrians, Hood Bridge is comparatively modern; before its construction the river was crossed by a ford.

STAVERTON
The Church 1889
21640

Legend has it that after founding a church near Penzance, St Paul de Leon sailed up the coast and then the Dart to found the church here. The first church, built from thatched wattle and daub, was succeeded by a small Norman structure and eventually by the present church, built on the orders of Bishop Stapledon in 1314.

STAVERTON, *The Church, the Interior 1889* 21641

The church interior was restored in 1877, an event which caused the Reverend Sabine Baring Gould (of 'Onward Christian Soldiers' fame) to rush back from London to prevent his ancestors' memorials being concreted over. The memorials were moved to Baring Gould's parish at Lew Trenchard.

▶ **STAVERTON**
The Bridge
1889 21643

Until the
14th century, the
only crossing
here was a ford.
A wooden
bridge was built,
but soon fell
into disrepair; a
new bridge was
built in 1413,
funded, as was
common at the
time, by the
church issuing
indulgences.

◀ **STAVERTON**
The River Dart and
the Old Bridge c1950
S817006

Staverton Bridge has seen
its fair share of incidents,
especially in the form of
floods; though less
common than they were,
these still occur. Perhaps
the oddest incident on
the bridge took place in
1436 when the vicar, Sir
John Laa, killed John
Gayne with a knife after
an argument. The Bishop
accepted that he had
been provoked, and let
him off!

▲ **DARTINGTON,** *The Church 1889* 21644

Dartington's original church stood in the grounds of Dartington Hall; this one was relatively new when the photograph was taken, having been consecrated to St Mary the Virgin in 1880 by Bishop Temple, who later became Archbishop of Canterbury.

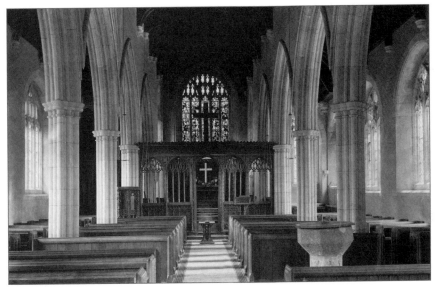

◄**DARTINGTON**
*The Church Interior
1890* 25425

The church was designed by John Loughborough Pearson, architect of Truro Cathedral, and has the same ground plan as the old 15th-century church. Stone from near and far was used in the construction: local stone from Shinner's bridge for the main fabric, Dartmoor granite for the font, Beer stone for the arcade, and Portland stone for the plinths on which the pillars stand.

BERRY POMEROY
The Church 1889 21635

At the time St Mary's was built in the 15th century, the lord of the manor was Sir Richard Pomeroy, who died in 1496 and is buried here in a tomb chest. He was a descendant of Ralph de Pomeroy, who came to England with Norman the Conqueror, and whose arms can still be seen on the church porch.

BERRY POMEROY, *The Church Interior 1890* 25421

The 42ft rood screen survived being defaced by Parliamentarian troops in 1640; a rather ungrateful gesture on their part, as Totnes was largely on their side during the Civil War. The 17th-century altar and rails seen here have been replaced and are now in the north aisle.

BERRY POMEROY
The Castle, the Banqueting Hall
1928 81156

The mansion was built within the walls of the 14th-century castle by Edward Seymour, Duke of Somerset, in the 15th century. Seymour, who was brother of Jane Seymour and later Regent for Edward VI, lavished over £20,000 on the mansion, but it was unfinished when he was executed in 1552.

TOTNES, *The Weir 1905* 53218

The weir, a mile up the river from Totnes Bridge, was built in 1581 to provide water for the town mills, and marks the end of the freshwater Dart - below here the river is tidal. On the far bank a salmon ladder can just be seen; these were built into many of the big weirs to give migrating salmon a better chance of reaching the spawning grounds upstream.

▶ **TOTNES**
*From the Exeter Road
1931* 84018

The story goes that in 1170 BC, after their defeat at Troy, the Trojans sailed here, led by Brutus, the founder of Britain. They followed the Dart upstream, and when they landed Brutus proclaimed: 'Here I stand and here I rest; And this place shall be called Totnes'.

◀ **TOTNES**
From the Mount 1889 21623

The Mount is still largely undeveloped today, its tree-clad slopes rising to the south west of the town. The valley of the Dart runs behind the church and diagonally leftwards across the picture. On the far left, the church at Dartington can just be seen through the haze.

TOTNES
Follaton Avenue
1905 53217

Follaton Lodge (right)
still stands, but nothing
else is today
recognisable in this
scene; Follaton Avenue,
once popular for a
Sunday afternoon walk,
is now Plymouth Road,
and built up on both
sides. Follaton House,
once the home of the
Carys, is now the
headquarters of South
Hams District Council.

TOTNES, *The Castle 1894* 33838

In AD 907, Edward, son of Alfred the Great, embarked on the building of a series of burhs, or fortified towns, as a defence
against the Vikings. One of these burhs was at Totnes, built on a high spur overlooking the ford on the Dart. The castle keep,
70ft in diameter, was built in the 12th century.

TOTNES, *North Gate 1890* 25412

Totnes became fully walled in 1215. There were four entrances: the East Gate, which still stands between High Street and Fore Street; the West Gate, which stood in the Narrows; the South Gate, behind the square on South Street; and the North Gate, in Castle Street.

TOTNES, *North Gate 1928* 81002

By the 19th century the North Gate had suffered from years of neglect (see picture 25412), and was in danger of disappearing altogether. Fortunately, it was restored to something approaching its original condition, as seen here.

TOTNES
Borough Park 1928
80993

By the early 20th century the Borough Council was worried that there were few public open spaces in town, and set about finding a site. They had to wait, but in 1919 were able to purchase some land from the Stearts Estate to build Borough Park. The bandstand and palm trees are long gone.

TOTNES, *The Guildhall 1906* 55255

The 16th-century Guildhall was built on the site of the priory refectory. The covered walkway in front was added in 1897, using the pillars from the old Corn Exchange which stood between the church and High Street. The exchange was built by Richard Lee, once Mayor of Totnes, and two of the pillars have his initials carved at the top.

▲ **TOTNES,** *The Parish Church 1896* 38229

The red sandstone parish church of St Mary was built by Roger Growdon and dedicated in 1450 by Bishop Lacey, whose name can still be seen on pub signs around Devon. The 120ft tower was completed in 1459; stone for the building was landed at a quay specially built at the bottom of the hill.

▲ **TOTNES**
The Guildhall, the Council Chamber 1896 38239

The wall on the left now has two boards bearing the names of all the Mayors of Totnes back to 1359. The oak tables are Jacobean, and were used by Oliver Cromwell and General Fairfax in 1646 to plan their strategy.

◄ **TOTNES**
General View 1890 25408

The roofscape of Totnes remains largely unchanged. In the distance is St John's Church, Bridgetown; the wooded hill to the right is now the large housing estate of Westonfields. On the horizon is the 643ft eminence of Beacon Hill, once used for signal fires and today, with its twin masts, still in the communication business.

TOTNES, *High Street 1896* 38226

The names on the shops may have changed since 1896, and the fashions moved on, but essentially this scene is little different from that of today, with one major exception - there is a total absence of cars.

TOTNES
High Street, Looking Down 1896 38225

While today many ground floor shop fronts have been modernised, some are preserved almost exactly as they were in 1896. A good example is the premises of Stephens & Hayman, Outfitters (second from the right). Today it is Rumour Wine Bar, and the frontage looks much as it did a hundred years ago.

TOTNES, *Butterwalk 1922* 73217

The Butterwalk takes its name from the days when dairy produce from the South Hams was brought into town and sold under the shade of the walkway. On the right was the poultry walk, cattle were sold in the square at the top of the High Street, and meat was sold in the main square down the hill.

▼ **TOTNES,** *High Street and Nicholas Ball's House c1960* T66114

Nicholas Ball was a wealthy Tudor merchant who made his money from pilchards and dried eels. His house at 16 High Street (right) is now home to Barclay's Bank. After his death his widow Anne married Sir Thomas Bodley, who founded the Bodleian Library in Oxford.

► **TOTNES**
Eastgate 1928 80999

The East Gate originally had two gates, one for carts and a smaller one for pedestrians. It was widened to its present configuration in 1837, and a lath and plaster false wall was built on the High Street side; this was only discovered during the £10 million restoration that followed the fire of 1991.

◀ **TOTNES**
Fore Street 1896
38222

The King William the Fourth (left) served not only as a pub but also as a bus depot - the smaller notice board here is advertising bus trips to Torquay for 1s. In 1902 it was demolished and completely rebuilt. The town's gas lighting was installed in 1837 – note the lamp standard on the right.

▶ **TOTNES**
The King Edward VI Grammar School, the Quadrangle 1931 84029

The Mansion House was built by Charles Welford between 1795 and 1808. It passed through several owners before being bought by the Grammar School for £187 in 1887. The school stayed here until 1972, when it moved to its present site.

▶ **TOTNES**

The W J Wills Memorial 1931
84019

William John Wills, born in Totnes in 1834, was a member of Robert Burke's ill-fated expedition to cross Australia from north to south. They succeeded - the first white men to do so - but three out of the four men, including Burke and Wills, died of starvation on the way back.

▼ **TOTNES,** *The Seven Stars and Portland House 1896* 38218

Several princes and future kings have stayed here while at Britannia Royal Naval College - hence the royal prefix. Portland House, on the right, became ye Old Oak Cafe, and was eventually demolished in 1936 to make way for Coronation Road. On the right are the rails of the spur that used to run down to the wharves.

▶ **TOTNES**

The 'Totnes Castle' at the Landing Stage 1896 38216

The coaches on the quay are courtesy ones from the Castle Hotel, waiting to pick up guests. This 'Totnes Castle' was succeeded in 1923 by another paddler of the same name, built at Philips' yard in Dartmouth. She had a long career before she was lost in a storm while being towed to Plymouth in 1967.

◄ **TOTNES**
*The Island
1889* 21625

The island was opened as a pleasure park in 1844. In 1971 Totnes was twinned with Vire in Normandy and the island was renamed Vire Island. On the left is a trading ketch, possibly loading cement from London onto the waiting railway wagons; on the return journey the cargo was often Symon's cider.

▶ **TOTNES**
The Landing Stage 1928
80988

The 'Compton Castle', which we
see here, was built by B Cox &
Company of Falmouth in 1914;
she originally had an open
bridge which was enclosed in
the 1920s. She plied her trade on
the river until 1962, when she
moved to Salcombe and became
a tea shop. She ended up at
Truro, where she was used as a
florist's and coffee shop.

◄ **TOTNES**
*The River Dart
and the 'Berry
Castle' 1922*
73224

The River Dart
Steamboat
Company was
known for its
paddle steamers,
but in 1922
embraced new
technology when
it bought the
'Berry Castle', its
first motor ship,
which replaced a
paddler of the
same name and
ran between
Totnes and
Dartmouth,
skippered by
Bill Rehberg.

▼ **TOTNES,** *The Seymour Hotel 1928* 80991

The Seymour Hotel was built by the 11th Duke of Somerset, who also built the church of St John in Bridgetown. In the 19th and early 20th centuries, Bridgetown was the height of fashion and the hotel did a roaring trade, but eventually it was turned into flats.

► **TOTNES**
*The River Dart
1931* 84020

Dutch, German and Scandinavian coasters visited regularly with cargoes of timber for F J Reeves, who imported their first cargo in 1903 and continued to do so for three generations. Turning the coasters round for the return journey was a tricky manoeuvre in such a confined space, and later a turning bay was cut on the east bank.

◄ TOTNES
The Bridge
c1955 T66048

The original bridge here was home to the Chapel of St Edmund (patron saint of bridges), 'founded by William de Kantelupe for the maintenance of a pryst to say masse and pray for his sowle in a chapel at the west end of ye bridge of Totnes'.

► TOTNES
The Bridge c1960
T66088

The old bridge had either four or six arches, depending on which old engraving you look at. This bridge was built in 1826 and designed by Charles Fowler, who also designed Covent Garden. It was a toll bridge until 1881.

▶ **TOTNES**
The River Dart c1965
T66116

By the late 1960s the RDSC had replaced their paddlers with three motor ferries: the 'Conway Castle', the 'Seymour Castle', and the 'Cardiff Castle', the latter skippered by Bill Rehberg, who served the company for 48 years. The last service ran in 1974.

◄ TOTNES
The Dartmouth Boat Leaving c1960 T66082

The 'Kingswear Castle' was built by Philips & Son of Dartmouth in 1924. She remained in service until the 1960s, and in 1967 was bought for £600 by the Paddle Steamer Preservation Society. She was taken to the Medway, and after a long period of restoration, finally sailed again in 1983.

ASHPRINGTON TO KINGSWEAR

ASHPRINGTON, *The Village 1905* 53221

The Sharpham estate was the major employer locally; many of the domestic servants came from Ashprington, and the estate workers were paid from the window of the Durant Arms (left). The pub was built in the 18th century, and later took its name from Richard Durant, who became lord of the manor in 1841.

DUNCANNON
*The River Dart
1896* 38235

It is estimated that 17 million tons of sand have been dredged from the bed of the Dart. Duncannon was the spot where many of the cargoes of sand were tallied before being taken off to use in projects such as the building of Torquay's sea front. Dredging ceased in 1983.

THE RIVER DART, *A Paddle Steamer 1889* 21620a

Apart from making day trips for tourists, and ferrying guests from the railway station at Kingswear to the hotels at Totnes, the paddlers performed another essential function - everyday transport for local people. The fares in 1907 were 1s 6d single and 2s 6d return for foot passengers, 1s single for bicycles, and 2s single for motorcycles.

SHARPHAM
On the River Dart
1898 42507

Sharpham House was designed in 1770 by Sir Robert Taylor, architect of the Bank of England, for Lieutenant Philomen Pownell, skipper of HMS 'Favourite', who had just received a reward of £60,000 for capturing a Spanish ship. Sharpham is a 'calendar house', with a window for every day of the year (and an enormous window-cleaning bill!).

SHARPHAM, *The Boathouse 1899* 44587

The 550-acre Sharpham Estate has been farmed for over 1,000 years. Today, it is famous for two things: cheeses, made from the milk of Jersey cattle; and Sharpham wines, which have even received the thumbs-up from French experts.

STOKE GABRIEL
The Church 1918
68536

The church of St Michael and St Gabriel was built in the 13th century, but only the tower remains from this time. The rest of the church was rebuilt in the 15th century. The yew tree in the churchyard is at least 1,500 years old.

STOKE GABRIEL, *The Quay 1918* 68538

Stoke Gabriel's traditional industries were all centred on the river - sand dredging, cockling, and salmon fishing. The row of poles on the beach here is for drying nets, which at this time were made from natural fibres and tended to rot if not dried thoroughly.

▼ STOKE GABRIEL
The Victoria and Albert Inn c1965 S366054

Starkey, Knight & Ford's brewery was in Tiverton, and their trademark black horses could at one time be seen all over Devon. Their beer is remembered with misty-eyed nostalgia by all who drank it; the brewery closed in 1965.

► STOKE GABRIEL
The River Dart c1965
S366059

Changing times on the river - by the 1960s boats were being used for pleasure rather than business. The yacht in the centre is a Silhouette, built by Hurley's of Plymouth, and one of the first mass-produced yachts that brought sailing within the pocket of Mr Average.

◄ **STOKE GABRIEL**
The Village c1965
S366159

The mild climate, fertile soils and long growing season of the South Hams mean that the area has always prospered agriculturally. The Dart valley, like that of the Tamar further west, has the added benefit of a sheltered microclimate which makes it ideal for growing fruit: in the background we can just see a couple of neatly laid out orchards.

► **GALMPTON**
School Corner c1960 G134002

Galmpton was once a centre of boat building. In the 19th century Brixham trawlers were built here, and in World War II Stan Hall built many launches for the navy. The prominent tree is the Jubilee Tree, an oak planted in 1897 to celebrate Queen Victoria's Diamond Jubilee.

◄ **DITTISHAM**
Beach Cottage
c1965 D34011

This beautiful cottage still stands, largely unaltered apart from a little pruning of the creeper on the walls and the trees to the left. Thatching in the South Hams was traditionally undertaken using reed from the shores of Slapton Ley, which was regarded as far superior to any other material.

◀ **DITTISHAM**
The River Dart
c1965 D34029

Although the
shores of the
estuary are heavily
wooded, such was
the scale of ship
building that as
early as the 18th
century there were
concerns about
timber reserves,
and timber,
particularly pitch
pine for planking,
was imported from
Scandinavia.

▲ **DITTISHAM,** *The River Dart c1955* D34004

The long pier was built to allow steamers to call at any state of the tide. The 7am ferry was always full with boatyard workers on their way to work in Dartmouth, but now the service runs only from March to October to cater for the tourist trade.

◀ **DITTISHAM**
The Church 1925
78382

The site of the church is
where Dittisham was first
settled - by a Saxon called
Dida in AD 765. St George's
has been here since about
1180, and was rebuilt in
the early 14th century. The
north aisle has stained
glass by Augustus Pugin,
who designed the
decoration of the Houses
of Parliament.

▲ **DITTISHAM**
The River Dart 1927
83090

Between the wars many ships were mothballed because of the depression and anchored in the estuary. Bibby Line, Prince Line, Lamport & Holt, PSNC and the Elder Dempster Line were among the companies who laid up ships. It is ironic that this vast stock of ships that nobody wanted was to prove crucial to keeping the supply convoys going in World War II.

▶ *detail from 83090*

DITTISHAM
The Quay, the River Dart 1925 78381

Out in the middle of the river, off Viper's Quay, is the Anchor Stone where, according to legend, any wayward or nagging wives from the village were tied as punishment. The Anchor Stone marked the northern limit of the deep water where big ships could be laid up.

DITTISHAM, *Binghay Woods and the Cottage 1925* 78379

Travelling from Dittisham to any location that was not on the river was a headache in the days before the car. In the late 19th century young Ewart Hutchings was educated at Upton School in Torquay, and to get there he had to take the ferry to Greenway, walk to Churston, get the train to Torquay and then walk to Upton.

▲ **DITTISHAM**
Yacht Racing 1925 78376

Deep water sailors will tell you that the only true test of man and boat is the open ocean, but racing on inland waters has its own challenges. The vagaries of tide and breeze on a narrow, restricted waterway such as the Dart estuary has left many a skipper red-faced for the lack of a little local knowledge.

▶ *detail from 78376*

DITTISHAM
Salmon Nets, the River Dart 1923
76470

Salmon fishing is recorded on the Dart as far back as Norman times, with many of the fisheries being mentioned in the Domesday book. There are records of over 4,000 salmon being taken on the Dart in a season, but the few boats that still fish today are lucky if their catches reach three figures.

TOTNES, *Greenway Ferry, the River Dart 1924* 76468

Hello Sailor! The foot ferry from Greenway Quay to Dittisham still runs all year round from 7.30am. Just up the road is Greenway House, built by Sir Walter Raleigh's half-brother Sir Humphrey Gilbert, and later home to Agatha Christie. In World War II the big house was commandeered for housing American officers, and Christie moved to the thatched cottage on the quay.

DITTISHAM
Greenway Quay
c1960 D34009

Around this time the foot ferry gave way to one capable of carrying six cars, but the experiment was not a success, and within ten years the service had reverted to foot passengers only.

DITTISHAM, *Greenway Quay c1960* D34010

Apart from the ferry, Greenway Quay has been fairly quiet, with the exception of two periods. The first was during the building of the seafront at Torquay, when sand dredged from the river was landed here; and the second was in the 1970s, when for a short time Browse Brothers' fleet used the quay for landing shellfish.

▲ **DITTISHAM**
The River Dart 1925 78371

One of the more unusual passengers to take the ferry in the 19th century was a donkey, who regularly travelled with its owner to Greenway with a load of cockles bound for Brixham market. The donkey must have had good sea legs and a sweet nature, for the boat was no bigger than the one shown here!

◀ *detail from 78371*

KINGSWEAR, *The Church 1890* 25292

In 1170, the same year that Thomas Becket was murdered in Canterbury Cathedral, William de Vasci deeded the church site to 'Richard the deacon and his successors'. Originally a chapel of ease to the parish church in Brixham, the church was dedicated to St Thomas; in 1837 Kingswear became a separate parish.

KINGSWEAR
From Watermouth 1898 42499

Although hilly - it rises to 586ft to the north east of Kingswear - the peninsula between the Dart and Torbay is very fertile, and it was this that attracted the Saxon king who founded the original settlement, then known as Kingston Vasci.

KINGSWEAR, *General View 1925* 78364

There has probably been a ferry of one sort or another plying its trade across the mouth of the Dart for millennia, but the first mention of one is in the Court Rolls of 1365, when it was run by one William Carey.

KINGSWEAR
*and the Mouth of
the River Dart*
1906 56627

The hill behind
Kingswear is known
as Mount Ridley; it
was the site of the
Redoubt, built in
1645 by Charles I's
men. It was taken
without a fight by
General Fairfax from
Sir Henry Carey in
1646, and then fell
into disrepair. In
1888 the seaward
wall was demolished
and a house was
erected on the site.

KINGSWEAR, *from Dartmouth 1890* 25275x

The jetty here was used for landing coal, some for bunkering for ships and later for the coal gas works at Torquay. The collier
'Similarity' was something of a fixture, making 257 visits to Kingswear before the advent of natural gas killed the trade.

◄ **DARTMOUTH**
Dartmouth Castle and Kingswear Castle c1875 3146g

Godmerock Castle (right) was built in 1501-02 on a little plateau just above the high water mark at a cost of £68 19s. It was not money well spent, for by 1717 a Colonel Lilly described Godmerock as 'useless and irreparable'.

◄ *detail from 3146g*

DARTMOUTH

DARTMOUTH
Old Mill Creek, the River Dart 1889
21609

This creek, upstream of the town, has seen many trades over the centuries. As the name implies, there was a mill here, and a limekiln (right). It was also the site of a smokehouse for Newfoundland cod, and more recently has been used for wintering pleasure boats.

DARTMOUTH
The 'Hindostan' and HMS 'Britannia' 1889 21598

These two ships were the forerunners of the modern Britannia Royal Naval College. The 'Hindostan' (left) arrived in 1864; the 'Britannia' was originally the 'Prince of Wales', but took the name of her predecessor on her arrival in 1869. 'Hindostan' was paid off in 1905, but 'Britannia' remained here until 1916.

DARTMOUTH, *The Royal Naval College 1906* 56626

The foundation stone of the college was laid in 1902 by Edward VII; the architect was Sir Aston Webb, who also designed the Victoria and Albert Museum. After the college's completion in 1905, the first commanding officer was Admiral Sir Jackie Fisher, who presided over cadets as young as 15.

▼ **DARTMOUTH,** *The Royal Naval Hospital 1906* 56621

The hospital was completed three years before the college proper; Sir Aston Webb's design included the use of covered colonnades to separate the wards and prevent the spread of infection. Today it houses the college's Royal Marine Band, and the Surgeon in Command's house is home to the commander of the college.

▶ **DARTMOUTH**
The Higher Ferry 1938 88632

The first floating bridge ferry ran here in 1831. It was steam powered, but this proved too expensive, and in 1835 the steam engines were replaced by two blind horses turning a capstan. This rather cruel state of affairs lasted until 1845, when steam was re-introduced. The steam age came to an end in 1959 when diesel ferries were introduced.

◄ **DARTMOUTH**
*A River Dart
Steamer 1930*
83030

At this time
practically all the
ships operating
out of Dartmouth
were powered by
coal. This was
brought in by
colliers and
transferred to
hulks moored in
the river, from
where it was
handled manually
by 'lumpers'.

► **DARTMOUTH**
The Quay 1899
44580

The row of shops
and houses was
built in the late
16th and early
17th centuries on
the New Quay,
which, as the
name suggests,
had only just been
reclaimed from
tidal mud. The
photograph was
taken from the
New Ground,
reclaimed in 1684.

DARTMOUTH
The Quay and the Harbour c1955 D7027

Some of the small boats here were almost certainly built at Lidstone's, whose South Town Yard started business in 1824. They specialised in building rowing boats and, later, small motor launches like the one in the foreground; in fact, the first motor boat in Dartmouth was launched by Lidstone's in 1910.

DARTMOUTH
The Promenade
c1960 D7086

Dartmouth Station is unique in that it never saw a train or even a length of track. Passengers disembarked at Kingswear and caught a GWR ferry to Dartmouth. A horse and carriage was laid on to take travellers on to Kingsbridge, but this was replaced by a bus service in 1917.

DARTMOUTH, *The Inner Harbour c1955* D7087

Behind the corner of the Boat Float, and distinguished by a white awning, is Parade House (centre), built in 1880 to replace the Assembly Rooms. In its original four-storey form Parade House was rather overpowering, but it lost two storeys to a German bomb in 1943.

DARTMOUTH, *The Inner Harbour c1955* D7018

The exuberantly decorated York House (right) was built in 1893 in a Victorian attempt to look Elizabethan - even down (or up) to the chimneys. During Regatta week the Boat Float doubled as a venue for swimming races.

DARTMOUTH
*The Promenade
c1955* D7015

The promenade
is actually North
and South
Embankment, both
built in 1882 and
the culmination of
Dartmouth's land
reclamation efforts.
When they were
completed the Boat
Float was enclosed,
leaving it only
accessible to small
boats.

DARTMOUTH
Royal Avenue Gardens
c1960 D7112

Once an island reached by
bridge from the Quay, Royal
Avenue Gardens were laid
out in 1880. The bandstand
was opened in June 1911 to
celebrate the coronation of
George V.

DARTMOUTH, *Foss Street 1889* 21602

This Tudor house stood on Foss Street, near its junction with Duke Street. The supports for the overhanging upper floors were finely carved wooden animals. But alas, they are no more to be seen, as the building was destroyed on 1943 by the same bomb that damaged the Parade House.

DARTMOUTH, *Mr Cranford's Shop 1918* 68630

The Cranfords came from Dittisham in the 1770s to set up a business dealing in tea and coffee. They soon diversified into other areas, notably newspapers, and in 1838 Robert Cranford, who later became Mayor, founded the Dartmouth Chronicle.

DARTMOUTH
Fairfax Place c1955 D7028

Fairfax Place was built in the 1880s, replacing some 16th-century properties. Oldreive Brothers (left) were highly successful butchers, supplying the 'Britannia' and visiting ships. Their Christmas display had four tiers of dressed poultry hanging from the outside of the first storey, and staff had to remain on duty overnight to prevent chicken rustling.

▼ **DARTMOUTH,** *Butterwalk c1960* D7110

This lovely Tudor building survived unchanged for 300 years before being badly damaged in the bombing of 1943. The exterior carvings and plasterwork were removed for safe-keeping, and the building was restored in 1954. Parade House (right) was demolished in 1980 and sensitively rebuilt, with a slate hung front, as the NatWest bank.

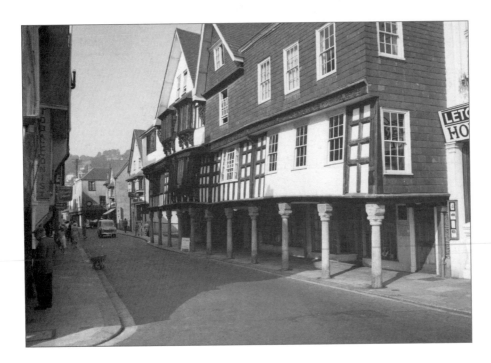

▶ **DARTMOUTH**
The Lower Ferry 1938 88631

The Lower Ferry was for a long time known as the Horse Ferry, as passengers often had to share the boat with horses. Originally rowed by two men with long oars, in 1870 it converted to steam when it was taken over by the Great Western Railway.

◀ **DARTMOUTH**
Bayards Cove
1938 88630

The first recorded quay here was in 1386, and the area is almost unchanged since the visit of the 'Mayflower' in 1620. Bayards Cove, which takes its name from the French 'bayart', meaning 'barrow', was most famously used as a set for the television series 'The Onedin Line'.

▶ **DARTMOUTH**
Warfleet Road 1934 86228

Warfleet lies downstream from Dartmouth on a small creek, and in the mid 19th century it was the site of one of the earliest villas in town. Gunfield House, now a hotel, took its name from One Gun Fort, where gunnery officers trained by shelling the opposite bank.

▶ **DARTMOUTH**
South Town 1930 83079

Dartmouth could quite justifiably claim to be responsible for the Portuguese national dish of salt cod, for in the 16th to 18th centuries local ships traded clothes and iron goods for Newfoundland salt cod, which was then taken to Portugal and exchanged for dried fruit and wine. Odd, the things history throws up.

◀ **DARTMOUTH**
From Mount Boone
1918 68615

In the centre is the church
of St Saviour; permission
to build it was first granted
by Edward I in 1286.
The tower is 14th-century,
and the rest was rebuilt by
the town corporation in
1633-37.

DARTMOUTH, *The Parish Church, an Old Door 1896* 38906

Despite the prominent date of 1631 in the centre of this door, the glorious ironwork depicting lions and trees is thought to date from the 13th century; the later date is probably that of a repair. The door now stands in the south porch.

▲ DARTMOUTH
From Warfleet Road 1934 86225

The three ships laid up here are the Bibby Line troopships 'Lancashire', 'Dorsetshire' and 'Somersetshire'. Moving laid-up ships could be a real headache for those concerned, as each one was secured to four anchors, and untangling the resultant cat's cradle of anchor chains was very tricky, particularly as the harbour master's barge had just the one hand winch.

◀ *detail from 86225*

◀ **DARTMOUTH**
The Town and the River 1931 84001

Coming round the stern of the troopships on the left is the 'Mew', the GWR ferry which ran to Kingswear from 1908 to 1954. On the right are Sandquay Docks, now a marina but once home to Philip & Son, who built many of the vessels that worked the estuary.

◄ DARTMOUTH
The View from
Kingswear c1960
D7076

The claiming of ships as
the spoils of war was not
confined to pirate
adventurers like Drake
and Raleigh: the predatory
motor boat (centre left)
looks suspiciously like a
World War II German E-
Boat. After the war several
of these were converted
for use as private yachts,
and one or two are still
sailing.

◄ DARTMOUTH
The Harbour c1905
42494a

Crossing the river to
Kingswear is the 'Dolphin',
the paddle steamer which
was the ferry from 1869
until she was replaced by
the 'Mew' in 1908. The
Royal Naval College might
still be under construction
in this picture, as both
training ships are moored
in the river.

DARTMOUTH
*SS 'Hawarden Castle'
1890* 25291

The mail and passenger ship 'Hawarden Castle', along with her sister ships the 'Dunrobin Castle' and the 'Norham Castle', were operated from Dartmouth by the Donald Currie Line from 1871-91. Despite being steamers, these ships still relied on sail for secondary power.

DARTMOUTH
The Regatta 1886 21652

'The Line' was one of the grand sights of early regattas - large yachts moored on the trots to form an honour guard for rowing crews. On the right is a gaggle of Brixham trawlers, many of them probably built on the Dart.

◄ **DARTMOUTH**
Castle Cove 1930
83082

Just visible on the far right at the top of the hill is the day beacon, an 80ft stone tower which marks the eastern side of the entrance to the estuary, as the entrance is almost impossible to spot from out at sea. The ship is either moving extremely fast or the photographer was using a long exposure!

◀ **DARTMOUTH**
General View
1889 21579

This is how the town looked before the building of the college. The berth in the centre of the picture was often used by mail boats taking news to the empire. Alongside this ship is a barge, probably bunkering coal from the coaling station just south of the Higher Ferry.

◀**DARTMOUTH**
Castle Cove 1918
68621

The Cove (see also picture 83082) is a popular bathing spot, but the diving boards, huts and sea-water pool are long gone, destroyed by storms.

DARTMOUTH
The Castle and St Petrock's Church 1889 21592

The first coastal fortress built specifically to carry guns, Dartmouth castle was built in 1481 on the site of John Hawley's original fortification of 1380, which had been constructed to deter Breton raiders. St Petrock's Church was built in the 17th century.

INDEX

NAMES OF SUBSCRIBERS

The following people have kindly supported this book by subscribing to copies before publication.

The Barrow Family, Ilsington

Geoffrey Barrow

J Alan Binns

To Arnold Brookfield Merry Xmas 2004

The Cain Family

William Chadwick

Margaret Clegg & John Clegg

George & Sheila Cook

Mr E Croston

To Dad love Susannah & Jessica

To my dear Daddy, Love from Thomas xx

Paul Davies

The Dixon Family, Bigbury

The Dyer Family

Mrs Anne Etheridge

David Fisher, Totnes

Mr K & Mrs S Foot, Totnes

Mr J Gillespie Snr

Mr A J & Mrs E Hanson

To Denis Harrison, 'A loving Husband and Dad'

Mr J & Mrs H Harrison

J O Inder & G E Inder

John & Debs, Riverside

In memory of Emily Johnson

Mr & Mrs D P Kilburn

The Knight Family, Paignton

Mr & Mrs P C Knight, Stafford

Ronald & Ena Lewis

Love to a special Mum, love Mary Lord

Mr A Mitchell

Michael & Barbara Mitchell

Tim & Kay Molyneux

Mrs D Mottram (nee Taylor)

Paul W Norley

The O'Connor Family

Heather Palmer 2004

Susan Palmer

Harry & Shirley Penny, Totnes

Melanie & Graham Robinson

William & Florence Rudd

Valerie Rushton

G P Smith

The Smithers Family

To my darling Steve on his 40th birthday

Brenda Stewart

Roger & Carolyn Taylor

To Uncle Tim with love Zoe & Family xx

In Memory of my Dad, Thomas Tucker

In memory of Delia & Fred Watson

In memory of Mr & Mrs J K Watson

In memory of M J Watson

David Whittaker & sons

Mrs M Wilcock & Family

FRITH PRODUCTS & SERVICES

Francis Frith would doubtless be pleased to know that the pioneering publishing venture he started in 1860 still continues today. Over a hundred and forty years later, The Francis Frith Collection continues in the same innovative tradition and is now one of the foremost publishers of vintage photographs in the world. Some of the current activities include:

Interior Decoration

Today Frith's photographs can be seen framed and as giant wall murals in thousands of pubs, restaurants, hotels, banks, retail stores and other public buildings throughout the country. In every case they enhance the unique local atmosphere of the places they depict and provide reminders of gentler days in an increasingly busy and frenetic world.

Product Promotions

Frith products are used by many major companies to promote the sales of their own products or to reinforce their own history and heritage. Frith promotions have been used by Hovis bread, Courage beers, Scots Porage Oats, Colman's mustard, Cadbury's foods, Mellow Birds coffee, Dunhill pipe tobacco, Guinness, and Bulmer's Cider.

Genealogy and Family History

As the interest in family history and roots grows world-wide, more and more people are turning to Frith's photographs of Great Britain for images of the towns, villages and streets where their ancestors lived; and, of course, photographs of the churches and chapels where their ancestors were christened, married and buried are an essential part of every genealogy tree and family album.

Frith Products

All Frith photographs are available Framed or just as Mounted Prints and Posters (size 23 x 16 inches). These may be ordered from the address below. From time to time other products - Address Books, Calendars, Table Mats, etc - are available.

The Internet

Already fifty thousand Frith photographs can be viewed and purchased on the internet through the Frith websites and a myriad of partner sites.

For more detailed information on Frith companies and products, look at these sites:

www.francisfrith.co.uk
www.francisfrith.com
(for North American visitors)

See the complete list of Frith Books at:

www.francisfrith.co.uk

This web site is regularly updated with the latest list of publications from the Frith Book Company. If you wish to buy books relating to another part of the country that your local bookshop does not stock, you may purchase on-line.

For further information, trade, or author enquiries please contact us at the address below:
The Francis Frith Collection, Frith's Barn, Teffont, Salisbury, Wiltshire, England SP3 5QP.
Tel: +44 (0)1722 716 376 Fax: +44 (0)1722 716 881 Email: sales@francisfrith.co.uk

See Frith books on the internet at www.francisfrith.co.uk

FREE PRINT OF YOUR CHOICE

Mounted Print
Overall size 14 x 11 inches (355 x 280mm)

Choose any Frith photograph in this book.
Simply complete the Voucher opposite and
return it with your remittance for £2.25 (to cover
postage and handling) and we will print the
photograph of your choice in SEPIA (size 11 x 8
inches) and supply it in a cream mount with a
burgundy rule line (overall size 14 x 11 inches).
**Please note: photographs with a reference
number starting with a "Z" are not Frith
photographs and cannot be supplied under
this offer.**
Offer valid for delivery to UK addresses only.

**PLUS: Order additional Mounted Prints
at HALF PRICE - £7.49 each** (normally £14.99)
If you would like to order more Frith prints from
this book, possibly as gifts for friends and family,
you can buy them at half price (with no
additional postage and handling costs).

PLUS: Have your Mounted Prints framed
For an extra £14.95 per print you can have your
mounted print(s) framed in an elegant polished
wood and gilt moulding, overall size 16 x
13 inches (no additional postage and handling
required).

IMPORTANT!

**These special prices are only available if you use
this form to order . You must use the ORIGINAL
VOUCHER on this page (no copies permitted). We
can only despatch to one address. This offer
cannot be combined with any other offer.**

Send completed Voucher form to:
**The Francis Frith Collection, Frith's Barn,
Teffont, Salisbury, Wiltshire SP3 5QP**

CHOOSE A PHOTOGRAPH FROM THIS BOOK

Voucher for **FREE** and Reduced Price Frith Prints

*Please do not photocopy this voucher. Only the original is valid,
so please fill it in, cut it out and return it to us with your order.*

Picture ref no	Page no	Qty	Mounted @ £7.49	Framed + £14.95	Total Cost
		1	Free of charge*	£	£
			£7.49	£	£
			£7.49	£	£
			£7.49	£	£
			£7.49	£	£
			£7.49	£	£
Please allow 28 days for delivery			* Post & handling (UK)		£2.25
			Total Order Cost		£

Title of this book . . . .

I enclose a cheque/postal order for £ . . . .
made payable to 'The Francis Frith Collection'

OR please debit my Mastercard / Visa / Switch (Maestro)
/Amex card
(credit cards please on all overseas orders), details below

Card Number

Issue No (Switch only)   Valid from (Amex/Switch)

Expires   Signature

Name Mr/Mrs/Ms . . . .
Address . . . .
. . . .
. . . .
. . . . Postcode . . . .
Daytime Tel No . . . .
Email . . . .

Valid to 31/12/07

Would you like to find out more about Francis Frith?

We have recently recruited some entertaining speakers who are happy to visit local groups, clubs and societies to give an illustrated talk documenting Frith's travels and photographs. If you are a member of such a group and are interested in hosting a presentation, we would love to hear from you.

Our speakers bring with them a small selection of our local town and county books, together with sample prints. They are happy to take orders. A small proportion of the order value is donated to the group who have hosted the presentation. The talks are therefore an excellent way of fundraising for small groups and societies.

Can you help us with information about any of the Frith photographs in this book?

We are gradually compiling an historical record for each of the photographs in the Frith archive. It is always fascinating to find out the names of the people shown in the pictures, as well as insights into the shops, buildings and other features depicted.

If you recognize anyone in the photographs in this book, or if you have information not already included in the author's caption, do let us know. We would love to hear from you, and will try to publish it in future books or articles.

Our production team

Frith books are produced by a small dedicated team at offices in the converted Grade II listed 18th-century barn at Teffont near Salisbury, illustrated above. Most have worked with the Frith Collection for many years. All have in common one quality: they have a passion for the Frith Collection. The team is constantly expanding, but currently includes:

Paul Baron, Phillip Brennan, Jason Buck, John Buck, Ruth Butler, Heather Crisp, David Davies, Louis du Mont, Isobel Hall, Gareth Harris, Lucy Hart, Julian Hight, Peter Horne, James Kinnear, Karen Kinnear, Tina Leary, Stuart Login, David Marsh, Lesley-Ann Millard, Sue Molloy, Glenda Morgan, Wayne Morgan, Sarah Roberts, Kate Rotondetto, Dean Scource, Eliza Sackett, Terence Sackett, Sandra Sampson, Adrian Sanders, Sandra Sanger, Jan Scrivens, Julia Skinner, David Smith, Miles Smith, Lewis Taylor, Shelley Tolcher, Lorraine Tuck, Amanita Wainwright and Ricky Williams.

Free Print – see overleaf